A Short Guide to Project Management of Engineers

Become a great project manager from an engineer's perspective

By **Geir Agustsson**

Table of Contents

Introduction

Project managers play an important role in a project life cycle. We all know why. They act as a facilitator between different disciplines within an organization, communicate with the client, bring together people to have all the important dialogues, manage the limited resources of the project, handle the finances, monitor the risks, ensure that the contract is respected, establish and enforce the project schedule and negotiate with relevant stakeholders if disputes arise.

Project managers are, in short, of huge importance for any project.

But they don't always perform. Sometimes they interfere to the point of halting progress. They stick their noses in where it doesn't belong, confuse the tasks at hand, fail to communicate relevant messages and become a bottleneck rather than a facilitator.

In this little book, the engineer is going to tell the project manager how and how not to manage a project as seen from his own perspective.

This might seem like a strange message. If the engineer is so good at managing a project, how come he isn't a project manager? Well, there's a good albeit a bit arrogant saying to explain that: Do what I say, not what I do. The engineer is more than happy to perform all the required analyses, write the documents, specify the production processes and perform all the required quality control needed to ensure a successful project execution. He's also perfectly happy to attend the meetings and enter into or initiate all the required dialogues. However, he doesn't want to handle the financials and book keeping, deal with the lawyers, suppliers and subcontractors, write detailed time tables, fight for production slots or move away from the technical aspects. The engineer wants to be a good engineer and he wants the project manager to be a good project manager.

If the project manager is the driver, the engineer is the engine. A bad driver can damage the engine so that it becomes less effective than it might be. And of course a driver cannot get very far with a damaged engine. This book is the engine talking to the driver and hopes that the driver is paying attention.

The aim of this book is to create a better work environment for everyone by pointing out what can be done better from the engineer's perspective. I sincerely hope that this book will encourage and strengthen such a dialogue.

People

People are different

Each individual is different. A project team is not a uniform mass of people with a uniform personality. One engineer is different from the next. Some like group work while others do not. Some want to know a lot about everything while others are more comfortable working with their own small piece of the puzzle without distractions. Some like the nerdy aspects while others are happier with the social element. Still others like both. Sometimes there is a large generation gap to consider. Men and women are different. Some are flexible, others need a fixed routine. Even the health of individual project team members can be of relevance for the project. Keep aspects like these in mind.

If a project manager has a lot of seasoned specialists in his team, his role will be different compared to a project manager with a lot of young, inexperienced people. While some people just need their path cleared to move on without knowing everything about how that is done, others need a lot of compliments and special attention and the feeling that they are involved in all decisions.

A project manager has to know how to get the most out of his team and will only be successful if he knows something about the strengths and weaknesses of each member of his project team.

It is futile to try to change personalities as they tend to be very stable over time. It is much better to accept people as they are.

Project managers need to know how to optimally use the strengths and weaknesses of each project team member. They should for example avoid putting shy individuals in socially demanding situations, such as supplier visits or high-profile meetings. They should not pile tasks on top of the easily stressed members of their project team. They should not stifle the efforts of the eager engineer who wants to break out of the box and try out new solutions or approaches.

A good project manager will do his very best to respect that people are different and that we all have strengths and weaknesses.

You and the engineer don't share a common world view

Engineers sometimes act like children in a toy store with their parent's credit card in their pocket. They want to play, figure out solutions, try everything out and spend a lot of time considering this and that. The engineer does not like to think about the financials of a project unless he has to. The budget only limits him and his creativity. The engineer wants to spend the time he thinks he needs to figure out the best technical solution.

The project manager may see things differently. He will often focus on the cheapest solution and to get it as fast as possible, while of course meeting the product or project requirements. This will make the client happy and the project budget look good. He wants constant progress without any side-tracking. He wants to aim for a solution on day one and work constantly towards it without delays.

These world views often collide. The project manager who understands this will figure out how to handle the situation. Other project managers – those who think that everyone thinks like themselves – will fail.

Your opinion is not the most important one

As project "manager" you are of course the captain of the ship. However, you can't sail a ship if the engine is broken or the hull is leaking. You can't shout "full speed ahead" and then realize that the anchor is down. It is one thing to know where to go and when you need to be there, another to know *how* to get there.

Your engineers are your engine. Their voice should have importance – sometimes more importance than your own. If they tell you that you are heading towards a dead-end, you should take this seriously. If they tell you that if you keep your course, your deliverables will be rejected by the client, take action. Ignore these voices and your project suffers. You are, of course, the captain of the ship. However, you can't run with a broken engine and should not steer the ship towards oblivion after being warned.

Forget your strengths, know your weaknesses

You are a project manager – the one in charge. You are fantastic in human relations, have an eye for planning, know your financials and wear a nice shirt. You know your strengths. You have participated in seminars and read books about project management. Nothing can stop you. The world is at your command.

Forget all about this. Your engineer doesn't care. He only wants you to provide him with the required ingredients so that he can do his own job. It doesn't matter if you are certified by five different organisations and have three different MBAs. Your task is to manage the project. If you fail this, you'll fail with five certifications and three MBSs just as much as someone with only his basic education.

Don't just dress nice. Talking nice is more important

A common trait among project managers is their over-ballooned sense of importance. Of course they are important, but without a functioning project team they are not going to succeed. The engineer knows this. If you treat your engineer with disrespect, he knows exactly how to deal with you. He will simply shut down in a very discrete way and prioritize other work.

Although you as a project manager practically have a dress code which includes a nice shirt, you can always trust that the engineer – the one wearing a torn t-shirt or a less nicer shirt - will appreciate a good joke or some juicy gossip from the big client meetings. If the engineer likes you, he likes your assignments.

Don't save the success stories for the bosses

Engineers are in many ways delicate people. They need an occasional reward for a job well done. This doesn't have to be a fancy dinner or an open bar, but something social will carry the engineer a long way. Find a way within your budget and time frame to give him this. Match your nice shirt with nice manners, and make a success visual and tangible. Your social relations with the engineers are important although you consider them introvert and "square".

This does not mean that you need to constantly dose out complements to people who are simply doing their job. This only means that if you are shining, it's partially because others are polishing your badge, and that you should share the glow somehow.

If the engineer feels you are riding on his back without acknowledging his efforts, he will abandon you, implicitly or explicitly.

Some project managers use every chance they get

to remind the engineers about the tight deadlines and tell them that the project is running late and is exceeding the budget. However, the same project managers will switch gear when the bosses come and tell them that everything is fantastic, on time and on budget. If you give the impression that this is the case, you will soon run out of success stories to tell your bosses.

Try to see through the eyes of others

As a project manager, you have certain responsibilities and are of course ultimately responsible for the overall success of your project. It is therefore tempting for the project manager to forget the views of others on the project. It is also tempting to forget that people are different – that while some thrive on problems that require quick solutions, others have the need to sink deep into the problems and dissect them into their smallest components.

Try to not only see your flock of engineers as manpower that can push whatever load you put in front of them but also to look at the problems at hand from their perspective. While some people tend to focus on their own personal progress, others tend to focus on cooperation and the overall progress. Some of us have "hard" or individualistic values (progress, solutions, deadlines) and others have "soft" or collectivist values (harmony, cooperation, mutual understanding). You can achieve a lot by tapping into these differences in values from the start and assign the tasks accordingly.

Trust should be earned

The project manager cannot handle all the project work himself. He will have to outsource most of the tasks at hand. This will free up his time for those tasks which need his full attention and belong to his core responsibilities.

However, trust should be earned. You don't want to hand over a task with a certain deadline only to discover that the person assigned to it didn't spend any time on it, or didn't have the required competences and didn't tell you about it.

The outsourcing process can end up in delays and poor quality and the project manager might not discover this until it is too late.

Trusting your project team is important. A person not trusted will become demotivated. With the correct combination of status reporting, discussions and feedback, you can allow people to earn your trust without getting the feeling of being monitored. Only then can you relax when the tasks are assigned to the project team members.

Motivation breeds efficiency

Do you wonder how you seduce your engineers to stay on your project and ensure that they work hard on it? Expensive team buildings, free merchandise and new equipment can of course be used to motivate, but lasting motivation is only created with ingredients such as enthusiasm, a feeling of progress and an atmosphere of constructive feedback.

Motivation is extremely important as it will breed efficiency. Your motivated engineers will do everything they can to dig into your assignments and complete them. They will enjoy having your well-earned trust and support. You will get an excellent return on every investment in motivation.

Planning

Mind the information overflow

Project managers and engineers need to manage a lot of information. There is of course the contract, the specifications, the standards, the clarifications from the sales process, the amendments, the technical requirements, the documentation and so on and so forth. The entire information package is more than one person can chew on. The project manager will have to entrust his engineers with the technical aspects, while the engineers will trust that the project manager is in charge of the overall formalities, reporting and the financial aspects, to name a few obligations.

However, the project manager will often feel like passing on all the information on his desk to his engineers. Meetings are called to discuss how certain aspects of the project management are being handled. Lengthy e-mails are sent to the engineers where assignments are hidden between the lines. Everyone is told to read an enormous amount of pages, filled with formalities. If the client changes his mind on something or adds a requirement, a waterfall of information is released upon all project participants. The project manager is eager to share all the details of his important work with the engineers, while often having no interest in the technical aspects that then get neglected.

Of course all this does not apply for all project

managers. Most in fact do a good job of containing the flow of information and paperwork so as to spare the engineers from an information overload. Others, however, show no mercy. They call into a series of lengthy meetings to discuss that which occupies their own mind.

The engineer is of course interested in more than just the technical specifications but there is a balance to be found on every project with every project team. Information is like liquid fuel. The information overflow will choke the engine. Lack of information will shut it down. An appropriate amount of information will keep the engine running at optimal speed.

"Flow" is the key to success

The project manager is a facilitator and as such an indispensable part of every project. He can ensure a steady flow of the correct information so that all of his project participants run at optimal speed. He can also stifle the flow of information, or create an information overload, and both will delay progress.

The project manager needs to find the perfect balance here and make sure everyone is in a "flow" – no more, no less. Flow is the key to a successful project. For some, all the information up front (when available) is the best way forward. For others, small doses of manageable information are more suitable. For most, the middle ground is the optimal amount.

Meetings are a waste of time, sometimes

Engineers and project managers have an opposite view on meetings. Some project managers consider meetings to be one of the most important tools in their toolbox. In their mind, meetings ensure a good flow of information, are required to align all stakeholders and necessary to follow up on progress.

Many engineers will, however, consider many – but not all – meetings as a waste of time. Sometimes meetings are all about listening to other people talk about details and specifics of their own work and problems – an often irrelevant ingredient to the work of other meeting attendees. The engineer does not feel the need to be called into meetings to talk about status or progress. Quite the opposite, he will consider such meetings a distraction and a waste of time – something that actually delays progress.

Of course, project team members often need to listen to each other to get a common perspective and exchange ideas. The project manager just has to remember that a 30 minute meeting takes a lot more than 30 minutes when everything is included: Preparation, getting to the meeting room, leaving the meeting room and getting back into action.

Meetings can be necessary and are often useful if they follow certain guidelines, like being kept relevant, short and to the point, with a limited number of well-prepared attendees and a strict agenda to follow. Good meetings *are* possible every time *if* these basic principles are adhered to.

If the project manager is in the awful situation of seeing lack of progress and overruns on the budget, he should consider other methods than endless meetings.

Don't get your beak stuck in the ground

Your weaknesses as seen by the engineer are, of course, obvious: You are not an engineer (even though your education and previous occupation was in engineering), you don't actually work on the technical problems and have a fantasy world picture of the actual work that needs to be done. Don't feel embarrassed about this because your job has nothing to do with engineering. Realizing something is the first step towards gaining control of it.

A good project manager will see things from a different angle, which is a necessary one. He will realize that he should have focus on the overall picture – to have the bird's eye and see all the movements occurring over a vast area. His engineers are on the ground, discovering, gathering and assembling the building blocks. If the bird gets his beak stuck in the ground, he will lose his overview without doing any ground work. Likewise, if those on the ground get thrown into the air they will lose contact with the ground without obtaining the overview of the bird.

Your colourful plan is useless

As a project manager you need to make project plans, preferably with many colours and a lot of lines. Your managers will like this. Your clients will too, those usually being represented with other project managers. Your engineers, however, do not care. Usually they won't even open the colourful plan, not even once. If they even know about it, you're in luck.

So how do your project engineers know when to do what and what is important? Here you will have to know your engineering resources. Some engineers need to work from a list where they can cross off tasks and make visual progress. Others only want to work on a few but important and complex problems and not be disturbed by an endless myriad of trivial tasks. Still others can do both. If you know your engineers, you'll know how to plan them without actually presenting them with a plan.

Your way forward here is to assign ownership to your engineers. They should get the feeling that they are responsible for a particular piece of the puzzle. You will rip them of this sense of ownership if you constantly breathe down their necks. Usually, if you get the feeling that your specific project constantly gets downgraded in their daily work or weekly plan, you would do well to realize that the engineer does not have the feeling of ownership in a meaningful way. If you succeed in assigning ownership to your engineers, you are one step ahead of all of your problems.

Don't create unrequired fires

The project manager is often faced with numerous challenges and changes in priorities. Perhaps the client called and wanted something ahead of schedule. Perhaps the factory wants to make some changes and requires some urgent input. You need to facilitate, provide answers and keep everyone motivated and moving. Thankfully, you oversee a flock of hard working engineers that can take the heat.

Remember that you cannot expect the same person to work on two tasks at the same time. Multi-tasking is a myth as your brain can only focus on one demanding job at the time.

Try to avoid creating unnecessary fires that require instant firefighting. The result of such a manoeuvre is several half-finished tasks and nobody gets what he wants. Prioritizing two tasks equally at the top of the list comes at a cost. You can of course make changes when needed, but don't pile all the "nice to have" tasks on top of the "must have" tasks and expect anything of value. Clear and direct communication that emphasizes actual priorities is always important and always appreciated.

Partnership

Mind your own business

Saying "mind your own business" to someone is usually a bit rude but it can actually be a quite useful reminder when understood literally. The project manager has a role to play – an important role. He is the facilitator – the captain of the ship or the driver of the bus – the one who keeps the propeller in the water, or the wheels in motion. He is, however, not a project engineer. He is not – or should not be – too deeply involved in the technical aspects of the project except when he is explicitly and purposely involved in them, or invited to do so. A project manager should not challenge design safety factors, request unrealistic production times, question the quality control of the engineers or throw technical bombs around. In other words, the project manager is responsible for the execution of the project plan, not for the project execution in detail.

Minding one's own business applies, of course, in both directions. The engineer should not try to challenge the project budget nor have client relations on his own terms and without the project manager's knowledge or approval. The engineer should not challenge the contract terms or request gold-plated solutions where others are required to stay within scope and budget.

Minding your own business does of course not mean that no-one shows anyone else's discipline interest or withholds useful comments when relevant. In fact, providing constructive feedback and comments can be a very important part of minding your own business. By doing that, your business is more likely to be getting the best possible conditions to thrive.

Be pro-active

The project manager should be pro-active towards his engineers. This might seem like an opposite to him minding his own business, and so it is. However, the project manager cannot make sure he's maintaining an optimal working environment for his engineers unless he's actively listening or seeking feedback. The project manager is the facilitator between all relevant stakeholders and if he fails to facilitate, the project won't succeed. The engineer will assume that he is informed and is working according to the latest specifications, budgets, plans and requirements. The project manager must pro-actively ensure that this is the case.

Don't outsource your core responsibilities

You, as a project manager, are a person with many responsibilities. You need to communicate with a lot of people, sit endless meetings, write and reply a lot of e-mails, talk a lot on the phone and manage the budget, the project schedule, the document register, your own project staff and all those pesky engineers.

But how can you reduce your workload? Well, for one thing an e-mail not sent is an e-mail not replied – hence one less e-mail to think about. A good plan will not require your full attention all the time to stay on track, so make a good plan. A realistic budget compared to the scope of work will also help. And so on and so forth.

However, what many project managers are tempted to do, and should not do, is to outsource their own core responsibilities. An engineer will quickly notice if his desk is suddenly filled with project management tasks, like following up on deliverables, obtaining production slots or communicating extensively with the client's project management. His technical responsibilities will as a consequence lag behind schedule and this will generate frustrations for everyone involved.

Outsourcing is often a very clever way to distribute tasks in the most economical way but if you take it too far, nobody wins.

Your project is only one of many

A project manager is seldom in a situation where he can take his engineering resources for granted. Often his engineers are juggling several projects and constantly changing from one to another. This creates a frustration for the project manager which can have several consequences, among others the feeling that constant meetings are required to keep the project on track and in focus.

What is often the result of constant delays as a consequence of constant shifts in priorities is that projects become delayed to the point of needing intense work at the very last minute to make the deadline. This is "firefighting" project execution – a situation where all projects are delayed and always in panic mode.

The project manager has to find a way to get out of this death spiral, where he can only hope for the best when his "fire" appears. Sometimes, top management will have to change its view on things, or the steering committee must be convinced of a new approach.

However, the engineers can also become useful here. They often have some flexibility in their day to squeeze in an hour here and there to ensure sufficient progress in order to avoid a "fire". The engineer will work for you if he sees the importance of doing that. He won't if you have been chasing him during the entire project for every little detail and harass him with meeting invitations every time you strike a thought.

Sometimes you must pull the necessary strings and overrule the priorities of the project team members or their managers. Try, however, to negotiate and motivate instead of just dishing out orders. This will be your best long-term strategy.

Is it you or the manager who has his head on the block?

Often the project manager is not the manager of his project staff, or at least not the engineers. The engineer has his own manager with whom he plans what to do and when. This can result in a conflict if the project manager wants many to work on his project but is only allocated a few.

Here the project manager often needs diplomatic skills to negotiate with the engineering managers. A project manager that is always in firefighting mode will tend to be behind schedule and at some point, the engineer managers won't listen to his requests for additional manpower. The manager who constantly undervalues the need for engineers will fail to provide the necessary resources.

The project manager and the engineering manager should from the start have an alliance that works for both parties and results in a sufficient supply of highly motivated engineers when needed. Both might have to make some adjustments to their "business as usual", but both are in reality aiming at the same goal and should be aware of that. In practice, *both* of your heads are on the block. You must ensure that this is never forgotten.

Do the bosses stifle your progress?

You as a project manager are often in a resource juggle. You need to manage limited funds and achieve unlimited success. Time is always in great demand but short supply. And of course you need people allocated to your project.

Some project managers feel that their human resources are constantly being sucked out of their project. The bosses – the group and department managers – starve your project by allocating all the required engineering resources to something else. How can you tackle this?

Engineers are often very autonomous creatures. They don't like constant supervision. Freedom is their favourite condition, and of course the associated responsibility. You can take an advantage of this. If you succeed in given your engineers a sense of ownership, you need not worry.

Besides this, engineers can often allocate their efforts on your project if they can convince their manager of the importance of this. You are a project manager – one of many who fill up the mailboxes in the company. Try to build an excitement around your project. If you can do this, you will have an army of people fighting the resource battle with you and even to some degree for you. In other words, you can often circumvent the bosses that stifle your progress but only if the engineers themselves feel like helping you.

You or them, or you *and* them

Engineers are in many ways a strange pack. They enjoy – really enjoy – talking about their work.

They will brag about a piece of programming code or how they obtained technical feasibility or something like this. You don't understand what is so fascinating about their talks amongst themselves. For you, the deadline was the most important achievement, not the software or machine or material manipulation required to meet it.

Don't feel any pressure to actually participate in the engineer's discussions with his fellow engineers. Likewise, don't ask the engineers to admire your minutes of meeting or contract amendments.

You are on the same boat, nevertheless. What you have in common is the client, the deliverables and the project in its broad picture. Men and women are different but still they come together to produce children and run a household. It's not a battle. It should be cooperation where each of us considers each other's strengths and weaknesses to cross the finish line – on time, on budget and according to specification.

The art of decisiveness

If the project manager changes the course of the project, others follow. If he drives off a cliff, all will perish. It is his judgment that decides the course ahead.

In order to make a decision, the project manager needs information from all project participants, including his engineers. He should have all relevant information to take the correct and informed decision.

However, this process can not only ensure that the correct path is taken but in fact stall the whole process. By taking too long to digest all the information or shying away from taking a decision, the project manager can delay progress in a significant way. The project manager will produce e-mails and meetings to make sure that the correct decision is taken but the net result it that no decision is taken and this hurts everyone involved.

The art of decisiveness is in obtaining a balance between gathering information and seeking feedback and to know when to move on. Sometimes this involves taking risky decisions with an uncertain return, and so be it.

To sum up

Being a good project manager can be a tricky business. Managing engineers can furthermore add to this trickiness. The engineer is usually an independent personality, often with strong opinions on how things should be done. Engineers are also a varied species with strong individual preferences, often reflected by their age, gender, education, previous experience and social background. Even their health can be factor to consider.

Your most important element should be confidence towards your own responsibilities and humility towards the tasks of the engineers. You'll get far by ensuring an open dialogue and good communications while making sure everyone has all the required information and are free from unnecessary disturbances and interferences.

APPENDIX

Copyright

Acknowledgements

First, I would like to thank my wife for her endless support and inspiration and for her useful comments when I was writing this little book. And my family deserves thanks for keeping me very busy at home and thereby for making me very aware of all wastes of time and conflicts of interest around me.

Second, I would like to thank those who helped me with this little book by giving me useful comments and suggestions. You know who you are! (I, of course, take full responsibility for any errors, or potentially bad or insulting advice in this book.)

Third, I would like to thank my employer for the last many years for never giving me a dull moment.

And last but not least, I would like to thank my friends and colleagues throughout my life. I have learned so much from you, and will continue to do so.

About the author

This author is an engineer with more than a decade of engineering work experience on his back. He is a married man with two children, and has a demanding job.

Combining family and work has perhaps been the most challenging work of his life, and has forced him to maintain a constructive attitude to all those little things that either distract or assist in the daily routine.